FLYING
START

FLYING SCHOOLS AND CLUBS AT BROOKLANDS
1910-1939

M.H.GOODALL

FLYING SCHOOLS AND CLUBS AT BROOKLANDS 1910-1939

Published in Great Britain by Brooklands Museum Trust Limited
© Copyright 1995 Brooklands Museum Trust Limited and M.H.Goodall
First Printed 1995
ISBN 1-900338 – 00 – 9

Designed by Quadraphic Design.
Printed in England by Ian Allan Printing.
Published by Brooklands Museum Trust Limited
Distributed by Brooklands Ltd
The Club House
Brooklands Road Weybridge
Surrey KT13 0QN England
(Museum open Tuesday – Sunday all year round except Christmas)
Telephone: (01932) 857381
Fax: (01932) 855465

FLYING SCHOOLS AND CLUBS AT BROOKLANDS 1910 – 1939

Brooklands is the birthplace of British motorsport and aviation. The record-breaking cars and daredevil drivers became legends in their own lifetime. What is probably not so well-known is that Brooklands trained the pilots and engineers who pioneered flying in Britain and who went on to become the founders of the Royal Air Force and of the aircraft manufacturing industries.

Many names spring to mind: A.V.Roe, Tommy Sopwith, Harry Hawker, John Alcock, Hugh Trenchard, Hugh Dowding and the Vickers trio Rex Pierson, Archie Knight and Percy Maxwell-Muller. The list is endless.

In the 1920's and 30's the flying schools and clubs, with the enthusiastic tuition of instructors such as Duncan Davis and George Lowdell, turned out scores of qualified pilots who, when war came, provided an invaluable source of aircrew for the Royal Air Force.

The author is to be congratulated for setting out the history of flying training at Brooklands in such a readable way and for finding such a fascinating collection of old photographs, many from the Brooklands Museum's own archives.

Many of us are perhaps more familiar with the story of motor-racing at Brooklands. I commend this book to those who would like to help redress the balance and learn more of the exciting days of early aviation on this historic site.

Michael

His Royal Highness Prince Michael of Kent.
Patron of the Brooklands Museum.

August, 1995

The Cabair Group of Flying Schools are delighted to sponsor this book – "Flying Start" in association with Brooklands Museum.

Cabair's own 'Flying Start' came just down the road at Fairoaks where its founder and still Managing Director first learnt to fly in 1963 and subsequently started Cabair in 1969. The Cabair Group, who offer private flying training for both aeroplanes and helicopters, now operates at various airfields with nearly 100 aircraft.

We hope this book may encourage you to take your own 'Flying Start' and find out for yourself the fascination and exhilaration of the air.

Designed by **quadraphic** DESIɡN©

 Printed on Brooklands Gloss 130g/m² supplied by MoDo Merchants

ACKNOWLEDGEMENTS Grateful thanks are due to the following individuals and organisations who have kindly given information and photographs used in this book:- Brooklands Museum • J.M. Bruce • The late H.F. Cowley • Cross and Cockade International • Anthony Hewlett • Hulton Picture Library • The late A.J. Jackson • Robin Jackson • Phillip Jarrett • Stuart Leslie • Dennis Manning • Montagu Motor Museum • Stephen Ransom • Richard Riding • Royal Aeronautical Society Library • Royal Air Force Museum Library • Royal Automobile Club Library

Thanks are also due to David and Jocelyn Barker and Borough Books.

Front cover illustration by Michael Stride of a Bristol Boxkite Biplane flying over the original aircraft shed at Brooklands in 1911.
Back cover illustration by the late Arthur Sturgess of a de Havilland Tiger Moth over the 1930 Brooklands Aero clubhouse.

FLYING SCHOOLS AND CLUBS AT BROOKLANDS 1910–1939

CONTENTS

FLYING SCHOOLS & CLUBS AT BROOKLANDS

1910-1939

Flying first came to Brooklands in September 1907 when Alliott Verdon Roe brought his canard biplane from the stables in Wandsworth, where it had been built, for trials on the finishing straight. It was not until 8 June 1908 that, after fitting a more powerful engine, he was able to make a *'hop flight'* of about 150 yards. Unfortunately the Clerk of the Course, E. de Rodakowski, was hostile to aeroplanes and put every possible obstacle in the way of Roe continuing his experiments. However, his trials at Brooklands, where he made many short flights towed as a glider behind the cars of friendly motorists, gave him the *'feel'* of flying and paved the way for his later success at Wembley and Lea Marsh.

At about the same time as Roe, J.T.C. Moore-Brabazon was experimenting with a fragile biplane built by the Short Brothers of Battersea and later brought his large Voisin biplane to Brooklands, but achieved little with it.

In January 1909 'The Motor' produced the following report on the potential of Brooklands as a flying ground:

"A survey of the ground enclosed by the great motor track at Weybridge affords reason to believe that British aviators will soon have at their disposition a large open, level tract of land, where training and testing will be both safe and easy. That Brooklands would form a useful aeroplane centre if the ground were made suitable we suggested in December last, and we are pleased to observe that our proposal is meeting with general favour. Major Lloyd, the new manager of the course, is of the opinion that the conditions are well suited to the needs of the aeroplanist. A few ditches will have to be filled in and some levelling will be required, but for the greater part the land would need no more than a good rolling. In fact, in some parts the surface would earn the admiration of the head groundsman at Lord's.

The extent and nature of the area available is indicated by the shading on the accompanying plan of Brooklands. Stretching from north to south is a broad belt of even ground, over which a motorcar can move comfortably, and over which, therefore, an aeroplane can easily be taken at a slow speed. When this has been prepared, there will be a straight run measuring more than three-quarters of a mile in length and from 250 yd. to 400 yd. in width, with space at each end for turning. Only two obstructions exist – Hollick Farm and a gravel pit. Neither can be deemed

to spoil the ground, because a very slight deviation from a straight line will take a machine on a clear course. In the middle of the main belt is a square tract, about 300 yd. in length and breadth, and as smooth and level as a tennis lawn. Such an ideal surface should render this area most valuable for getting up speed in order to leave the ground, since it permits a turning radius of 450 ft. which should be ample

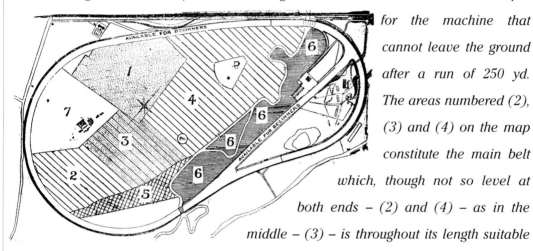

for the machine that cannot leave the ground after a run of 250 yd. The areas numbered (2), (3) and (4) on the map constitute the main belt which, though not so level at both ends – (2) and (4) – as in the middle – (3) – is throughout its length suitable for coming to earth. It possesses the great advantage of being entirely open and far removed from trees and is, moreover, adjacent to an area quite as large on which flights can be made and where machines can be brought safely to ground if it should become necessary to alight. On the east of the River Wey there lie meadows which are certainly smooth enough for a landing, the part south of the paddock being, indeed, used at race meetings as the members' car enclosure. Further, there is a large acreage (1) under cultivation over which even low skimming flights could be made and where a landing could in need be made, though compensation would

have to be paid if any damage were caused thereby. Since, in addition, the strip marked (5) could be prepared, there remains only the area marked (7) which could not be included in the aeroplane ground, its surface being too rough to enable it to be levelled without considerable expense. Expert opinion is now being collected, and if those for whom the ground will be laid out express themselves satisfied with the surface, this country will soon be the richer by an enclosed aeroplane ground within easy reach of the metropolis and where, therefore, successful flights will come under the close observation of the Press, which is a factor that will count for much in working the nation up to a high pitch of enthusiasm.

In explanation of Farman's dissatisfaction with Brooklands, it must be remembered that he regarded only the track itself, without giving consideration to the broad acres enclosed within the cement road. In light airs both the railway and finishing straights, which each provide a clear run of three quarters of a mile, are ideally adapted to the use of budding aviators, even though the complete circuit is not suitable for a course of flight such as Farman had in mind. It is well, also, to remember that Farman inspected the racecourses which lie within metropolitan influence, and came to the conclusion that they were not quite suited to aeroplane experiments.

Brooklands is quite a suitable ground where aeroplanes could disport themselves near London and for this reason it is very much to be desired that it will meet with the favour of aeroplanists themselves."

Nemo

Aviation then languished at Brooklands for something over a year until George Holt Thomas persuaded the Locke Kings that the new sport of aviation would give a great boost to the attraction of the Brooklands Motor Course. He arranged that the very successful French pilot, Louis Paulhan, should come to Brooklands to give an exhibition of flying. A piece of land of about 30 acres was cleared and a small shed was built. The flight took place on 29/30 October and 11 November 1909 in front of considerable crowds – a new attraction for Brooklands had now been born. Within a few weeks a Manager, sympathetic to flying, Major Lindsay Lloyd, was appointed. The ground was cleared and two hangars were built for rent at £10 per month. In November Lindsay Lloyd was sending out the following about the facilities available at Brooklands:

"With reference to your application for facilities for exercising an aeroplane at Brooklands, I beg to inform you that we are proposing to proceed on the following lines:

We will erect and maintain a suitable shed for each tenant and let same for the rents mentioned below. For these payments the tenants will have the exclusive occupation of the sheds and the right to use the interior of the track as an aviation ground upon all occasions except when the track is required for race meetings or when it would be, in our opinion, undesirable to have both aviation and motoring proceeding at the same time.

Aviators will have the right to use the ground already specially levelled and pre-pared, and to pass over the other portions inside the track which are cleared, and over which it is intended by degrees to extend the levelling and smoothing.

The *'Flying Village'* at Brooklands expanded rapidly and by the end of May 1910 17 hangars had been built and occupied by a total of 22 machines, thus:

Hangar 1 – Charles Lane
2 Lane Monoplanes

Hangar 2 – C.A. Moering
Voisin Biplanes

Hangar 3 – H.J.D. Astley
Lane Monoplane
Lionel Mander
Blériot Monoplane

Hangar 4 & 5 – Humber Ltd.
2 Humber Monoplanes

Hangar 6 – Neale
Neale Monoplane

Hangar 7 – Graham Gilmour
Blériot Monoplane

Hangar 8
Grégoire–Gyp Monoplane

Hangar 9 – Alan Boyle
Avis Monoplane &
Howard Wright

Hangar 10– Jack Humphreys
Humphreys Monoplane

Hangar 11 – Petre Brothers
Petre Monoplane

Hangar 12 – Trier & Martin
Monoplane

Hangar 13 – Carpenters Shop

Hangar 14 – A.V. Roe
3 Triplanes

Hangar 15 – Collier
Collier Monoplane

Hangar 16 – C. Graham-White
Farman Biplane

Hangar 17 – British & Colonial
Aeroplane Co. (Bristol)

Hangar 18 – Mann & Welling
Monoplane

The provision of workshops and preparing works for tenants will be a matter for consideration, and proposals in regard to this will be entertained.

For the rent of each shed and the facilities above described, each tenant will be charged either –

1. £100 per annum, payable in advance on signing an agreement; or

2. £10 a month, payable monthly in advance for an agreement of not less than six months' duration.

The construction of sheds is being proceeded with, and three sheds are expected to be ready in a fortnight, but other sheds will be built within four weeks of arrangements being made with intending tenants and preference will be given in the order of application.

The satisfactory experience of the last few days, and M. Paulhan's expression of opinion on the subject, show that the Brooklands ground, as at present laid out, is eminently suitable for aviation, and that the improvements now being made will render it still more valuable for this purpose.

I shall be glad to hear from you at your earliest convenience whether you wish to become a tenant on the terms mentioned above."

By the end of 1909 three or four owners had rented hangars and several more had expressed interest.

By April 1910 flying was in full swing with Lane, Blériot and Humber monoplanes, a Voisin biplane and an A.V. Roe triplane on the site.

The earliest arrivals to commence flying at Brooklands from January 1910 onwards had learned to fly and gained their certificates in France at Pau & Mourmelon. These included Charles Rolls, Claude Grahame–White, Graham Gilmour and Gustav Hamel.

Many others who arrived a little later were self–taught after one or two trial

The Aviation Village at Brooklands in about 1912 - the Blue Bird Cafe is in the middle of the photograph

flights with those who had already qualified. Minor crashes were very common but with the slow speeds and very low wing–loading, serious injuries were quite rare during practice. Well–known pilots who learned in this way were James Radley who gained his pilot's certificate on 14 June 1910, Alan Boyle, G.A. Barnes, A.V. Roe, H.E. Watkins, Tommy Sopwith, O.C. Morison, James Valentine, H.J.D. Astley and Robert Macfie.

Between June 1910 and January 1911 eleven Royal Aero Club certificates were awarded to pilots who had had private tuition at Brooklands on an 'ad hoc' basis. Tommy Sopwith was typical of the wealthy young men who could afford to buy an aeroplane, take it out, smash it, walk away smiling and then buy a replacement.

After the first rush of amateur enthusiasts had taken to the air, the professionals came on the scene and the first flying schools were set up.

THE
LANE SCHOOL

1910

First off the mark seems to have been the Gliding School of Charles Lane which was established at Brooklands in the spring of 1910. Lane built a biplane glider of Farman type and laid down a starting rail on the hillside below the public grandstands. One of his first pupils was Mrs. Gavin – by July 1910 she was making solo flights and earned the right to be called the first English lady aviator. At the time it was reported that she was about to start work with a power–driven machine; she may have done so, but there is no record of her subsequent flying career.

LANE'S GLIDING SCHOOL, now in daily operation at Brooklands, the aviation centre; thorough practical tuition in flying, without danger or risk. Come and see, or full particulars sent on request to THE MANAGER, Lane's Gliding School, Brooklands, Weybridge.

The manager of the Lane School was Eardley Billing, the brother of Noel

Pemberton Billing. He and his wife also ran the Blue Bird Cafe for the benefit of the fast–growing community of aviators. The School occupied shed No.1.

The Lane School subsequently gave instruction on powered aircraft, including the monoplanes and biplane designed and built by Charles Lane. One of their best known pupils was Cecil Pashley who trained on a Blériot monoplane and went on to form his own flying school at Shoreham.

The Lane School's monopoly at Brooklands did not last long. In September 1910 Hewlett & Blondeau, British & Colonial (Bristol) and Neale opened their doors to pupils.

Flight simulation has always been considered important as shown by this Eardley Billing Oscillator at Brooklands, c. 1911/12.

The 'Blue Bird' was one of early aviation's popular meeting places. In the summer Mrs. Billing served her famous 'Teas' outdoors. Nearby (far right), stood the world's first aviation ticket office catering to Brookland's joyflighters.

Mrs. Gavin on the Lane Glider on Members' Hill just below the grandstands

THE
HEWLETT & BLONDEAU
SCHOOL

1910-1912

Mrs. Hilda Hewlett, wife of the well–known Victorian novelist, Maurice Hewlett, was an early devotee of the motor bicycle craze and graduated from them to the motor car. Always eager to tackle new challenges, she went to learn to fly at the Farman School at Mourmelon in the early part of 1910. In order to hide this unladylike pastime from her friends (and perhaps her husband) she adopted the pseudonym of Miss Grace Bird. While there she met another pupil, Gustave Blondeau who, after some eight years in the automobile industry, had decided that his future should be in aviation.

Gustave Blondeau on his Farman Biplane

He told Hilda Hewlett of his burning ambition to become a pilot and aeroplane constructor. She agreed to give him financial backing if he would take her into partnership. They decided that there was great potential in England where flying was in its infancy. They therefore purchased a Farman biplane which they brought to Brooklands and named it *'The Blue Bird'* after the play written by her husband's great friend, Maurice Maeterlinck.

The Hewlett & Blondeau Flying School opened in September 1910 in shed No.32 and Blondeau commenced giving flying lessons to a growing band of enthusiasts which included his partner, Hilda Hewlett. On 29 August 1911 she became the first English woman to gain the Royal Aero Club's Pilot's certificate (No.122) and thereafter was the second instructor of the school. One of her first pupils was her son who eventually became a well–known pilot in the Royal Naval Air Service and the Royal Air Force.

Mrs. Hilda Hewlett at the controls of the Hewlett & Blondeau Biplane

One of their pupils, Maurice Ducrocq, a Frenchman, wrote the following appreciation of the Hewlett & Blondeau School:

"As an aviator I occupy a unique position. Accident of birth has made me a Frenchman, accident of business has kept me in England; the result of these two accidents and an intense desire to conquer the air has been that I am the only

Frenchman who has taken his pilot's certificate in this country. From start to finish I have accomplished my desire in twenty lessons, and I greatly doubt whether France, far in advance as it is of England, could have served me better. I ought to add here that, before my first lesson, I had never been in an aeroplane and had had no previous experience on gliders or oscillators, and, perhaps also, that I

> THE ONLY SCHOOL WHICH HAS NEVER HAD A
> SMASH NOR DAMAGED AN AEROPLANE,————
>
> **FIRST** Established School in England
> **FIRST** to pass an Army Officer for R.Ae.C. Certificate
> **FIRST** to pass a Woman for R.Ae.C. Certificate
> **FIRST** to pass a Pilot in Two Lessons
>
> **HEWLETT & BLONDEAU** (Brooklands, Weybridge)
> A Good Teacher means Safety and Rapidity. **£75** (Inclusive of breakages)

came into the practical part of the business with an open mind and a good deal of determination.

I began operations by a close survey of all schools and so-called schools of aviation in England. I mention no names, but there is no harm in saying that last August there were no schools actually in being within easy reach of London. One there was which had neither aeroplane nor pilot; another had an aeroplane but no engine; another had an engine but no pilot; another, even others, had insufficient engines, or planes which declined (very properly) to take the air. All this was most unsatisfactory to my mind. I was prepared to pay and pay well for instruction but not for nothing. Then, by accident, on the telephone I heard that a man had produced a Farman at Brooklands, had started the Gnome, that capricious spinning monster, at the first turn of the propeller, and made a fine flight. This, I heard, was his début in England. Having made enquiries I went to M. Blondeau at Brooklands with my desires and proposals.

I found that he was in partnership with Mrs. Hewlett whom he is also teaching to fly and that they were prepared to teach me from that moment. My lessons began

immediately, with the result that I passed the Royal Aero Club tests for my pilot's certificate on 21 October in a wind varying from 12 to 20 m.p.h.

The method is simple, and the manner of tuition is quiet and sympathetic.

M. Blondeau is a Frenchman, but speaks English, and has lived several years on this side of the Channel. He has had eight years in the construction of motors, and drove one of his own make in the Paris to Madrid race. He went over to the Farman School last January with Mrs. Hewlett and while learning there he spent his time in the workshops actually working himself. He also studied the Gnome near Paris. He is a very quiet man, hardly ever making a remark unless it is asked for; he neither loses his head or his temper. He can't be made to hurry. It was quite a joke at the Lanark meeting: the officials found out that it was no good 'fussing round' so they let him alone to come out when he was ready.

Mrs. Hilda Hewlett in flying kit at the rudder of her biplane

When he first came to Brooklands there were not many who flew out daily as they do now, and the older dwellers of the place were inclined to be patronising; they told him the Gnome didn't like the air of Brooklands, that the eddies were very bad and dangerous, and that a Frenchman had been there three months and then left because as a flying ground it was a death-trap. M. Blondeau, like Brer Rabbit, 'kept on saying nuffin'. He is not a showy pilot; he never does things to amuse the

public, but he loves flying on his own machine as he is certain that the motor and the plane are as safe and true as they can be made, in every detail. He leaves this to no mechanic; he has none. He does all tuning up himself and verifies every wire.

His method of teaching is as follows: every morning or evening, as the wind may allow, the pupil is taken up. He has all he can do to sit tight and keep his raptures to himself for the first two or three days. The engine purrs like an enormous cat, but with the regularity of a clock; there is a rush along the ground, then a steady lift when one becomes insensible to speed, conscious only of a strange exhilaration and an ampler air. For my first lesson I was deliberately taken to a considerable height and across country for, as was explained to me afterwards, it is good that the pupil should lose any sense of fear he may have and learn the possibilities of his new and wonderful faculty. After two or three days' experience of the sort, when my ecstasies were sobered down and my pulse steadier, I was taken day by day round the course at a lower altitude for by now I was prepared to give my attention to the machine and its working rather than to my own sensations. After three or four lessons I was allowed to touch the lever and let the machine 'feel my hands' and then it was that, with that lucidity and absence of fuss which marks Blondeau out as a born teacher, he taught me all I now know. After eleven lessons I began to fly in straight lines up and down the aviation ground, at first skimming the ground, then leaving it for short bouts,

PASSENGERS TAKEN UP
FROM £5.
AND **PUPILS TAUGHT** ON
FARMAN BIPLANE every suitable day.
PARTICULARS ON APPLICATION.
G. BLONDEAU, BROOKLANDS, WEYBRIDGE.

lastly in the air. In twenty-one lessons I was passed by the Aero Club. I do not hesi-tate to say that I could not have been taught better or more economically in England or anywhere else. I should be more than ungrateful if I did not testify to M. Blondeau's efficiency and patience and I think I may add that I am the first pupil of any aviation school in this country to qualify by examinations, and that certainly I am the first at Brooklands."

Hewlett & Blondeau next started selling aeroplane engines and spares, and building complete aeroplanes for re-sale. When they grew out of space in their Brooklands hangar they moved to a building in Clapham and eventually to a larger factory at Luton where they produced considerable numbers of aeroplanes during World War I.

Well-known pilots trained by Hewlett & Blondeau included Maurice Ducrocq, Spencer Grey and B. Graham Wood. A total of 13 Royal Aero Club certificates were issued to their pupils by the time the school closed down early in 1912.

Three Farman-type biplanes were built by Hewlett & Blondeau for use by the Vickers Flying School as their numbers 19, 20 and 21.

The Hewlett & Blondeau Biplane outside the sheds at Brooklands with a Howard Wright Biplane in the background

Tuning up for Flight, Brooklands Flying Ground. A.S. No.12.

THE
NEALE SCHOOL
1909–1911

JV Neale was one of the earliest British aeroplane constructors and his first small monoplane appeared at Dagenham in 1909. It was underpowered with its 9 h.p. motor-cycle engine and was not successful. Neale had a workshop in Baker Street, Weybridge, and from here appeared a further monoplane later in 1909. It took part in the 1909 Blackpool Aviation Meeting and was originally powered by a 24 h.p. E.N.V. engine. It crashed at Brooklands on 21 May 1910 and was rebuilt with substantial alterations, including the fitting of a 20 h.p. J.A.P. engine. It was still being flown at Brooklands at the end of 1910.

Neale's next design, the No.7 Biplane, appeared in the summer of 1910 and made its first flight on 1 August. At first sight it appeared to be a conventional

The Neale 7 Biplane.
Bertie Rippen is the pilot.

Farman-type but, in an attempt to avoid the Wright Brothers' patented wing-warping lateral control, the Neale 7 was fitted with rudders at each wing tip. No fin and rudder of the conventional type were fitted. The No.7 was used to train the Neale School's only known pupil, Bertie Rippen, who continued to fly with Neale as his instructor during the autumn. Rippen does not appear ever to have gained his Royal Aero Club certificate and the Neale School does not seem to have survived beyond early 1911 when it gave up the lease of shed Nos. 6 and 36.

THE
BRISTOL SCHOOL

1910-1914

I n September 1910 the British & Colonial Aeroplane Company opened its first *'Bristol'* flying school at Brooklands – this went on to be the most successful school in Britain prior to World War I. Out of 664 pupils trained up to 4 August 1914, no less than 182 gained their pilot's certificate at the Bristol School at Brooklands.

The company first went to Brooklands in April 1910 when they attempted to fly a Zodiac biplane which they had imported from France. Despite modifications it steadfastly refused to leave the ground. It was therefore decided that they would

A Bristol Boxkite at Brooklands

Above: A Bristol Boxkite at Brooklands with farm buildings in the background

Above right: A group of Bristol School pupils and instructors

design their own aircraft in future and G.H. Challenger was appointed chief engineer and designer. His first design was a modification of the Henri Farman pusher biplane. The Bristol Boxkite eventually became one of the most successful training aeroplanes ever built. The first of the Boxkites to be completed was fitted with one of the first 50 h.p. Gnome rotary engines to be released for export from France and was allocated as initial equipment of the new Bristol School at Brooklands. A second Boxkite was received in November 1910.

The impressive record of the Brooklands School soon led to the formation of further schools at Bristol, Salisbury Plain and Eastchurch.

The first Bristol Brooklands–trained pilot to obtain his Royal Aero Club certificate (No.28) was L.F. Macdonald on 15 November 1910. Three more certificates were gained by Brooklands pupils of the Bristol School before the end of 1910.

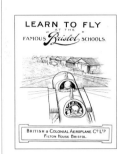

The success of the Bristol School was due to the skill and painstaking tuition provided by the instructors, including Busteed, Gordon England, Jullerot, Merriam, Pixton, Pizey and Sippe, and the excellence of the aircraft used. The Bristol Boxkite provided the ab initio training and pupils then often graduated to Bristol Coanda and Bristol Prier Monoplanes. During their four years at Brooklands the Bristol School lost only two pupils in accidents.

Above left: A Bristol Prier Monoplane used by advanced pupils

Left: A group of Bristol School pupils and instructors

Many of their Brooklands-trained pupils went on to achieve distinguished careers in military and civil aviation, e.g.

	Cert No.
Archie Knight	60
Gordon England	68
Harold Blackburn	79
Herbert Sykes	95
C.R. Brooke–Popham	108
Brigadier–General David Henderson	118
Warren Merriam	179
C.A.G. Longcroft	192
Sir A. Bannerman	213
Sidney Pickles	263
R.H. Barnwell	278
P.B. Joubert de la Ferte	280
Major E.B. Ashmore	281

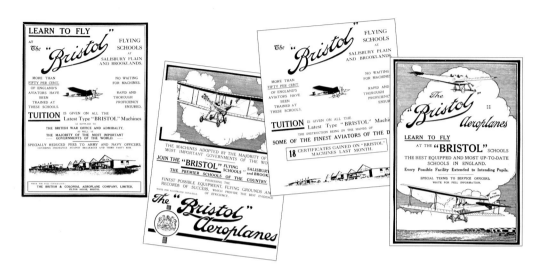

The Bristol School operated from sheds Nos. 17, 34, 35 and 36 and, at the outbreak of war in August 1914, these were turned over to the Royal Flying Corps which then became responsible for all flying training at Brooklands.

Getting ready for a day's flying – wheeling out a Bristol Box from its shed

THE
HANRIOT
SCHOOL

1910-1911

One of the earliest French aeroplane manufacturers was the father- and-son firm of Hanriot. The company specialised in the construction of monoplanes, several of which were imported into Britain. In the autumn of 1910, J.H. Thomas opened the Hanriot Flying School at Brooklands, based in shed No.19. Their first pupil was Keith Davies who gained his certificate (No.22) on 11 October 1910. The next to qualify was E.V.B. Fisher on 2 May 1911 and he thereafter remained as an instructor at the School until it closed at the end of 1911.

The Hanriot School was in full swing during 1911 and amongst the pupils who learned to fly on the old Hanriot monoplane *'Henrietta'* were Messrs. Gordon

An Hanriot Monoplane at Brooklands

Bell, Henry Petre and Gnosspelius. This monoplane had the peculiarity which seems to have been unique in that it could be flown *'cabre'* (tail down) without becoming unstable; when too *'cabre'* it simply subsided gently to earth without sideslip.

During its relatively short operational life the School had some eight pupils of whom three became well-known pilots (Hubert Oxley, Gordon Bell and H.A. Petre). Jack Humphreys, *'The Mad Dentist'*, was also a pupil but does not seem to have gained his certificate.

THE
AVRO SCHOOL

1910-1912

A V Roe, the earliest of the Brooklands pioneer airmen, opened a flying school at Brooklands in October 1910, having gained his Royal Aero Club certificate (No.18) on 26 July 1910 in his Roe Triplane. The School occupied sheds Nos.6 and 15 and used only Avro machines for tuition – these included the Roe IV Triplane, the Type D Biplane, and the Type E Biplane.

Below left: The Roe IV Triplane - initial equipment of the Avro School at Brooklands

Below right: The Avro Type D Biplane

Flying was taught until a full certificate was obtained at an inclusive fee of £50. Joy-riding flights were also offered.

The first pupil to gain his certificate was Howard Pixton on 24 January 1911. Eleven further certificates were awarded to pupils before the School closed down in about August 1912. Notable pilots trained by Avro included Ronald Kemp, Freddie Raynham, S.V. Sippe and Louis Noel.

The Avro Type E Biplane at Brooklands

THE
GRAHAME-WHITE
SCHOOL

1910-1911

In the autumn of 1910 the great showman and pilot, Claude Grahame-White, came to Brooklands and opened an aviation school. However, the environment at Brooklands seems not to have suited Grahame-White, perhaps there was too much local competition, and by February 1911 he had departed to Hendon where he set up the great aviation ground and factory which were to make his fortune.

The first and only pilot to be trained at the Brooklands School was C.H. Greswell who gained his certificate (No.26) on 15 November 1910. The aircraft used were a Grahame-White Biplane and probably a Henri Farman Biplane. The sheds used were Nos. 16, 24 and 25.

A Grahame-White
Biplane at Brooklands

THE
LD GIBBS
SCHOOL

1910

One of the first British pilots to gain a Royal Aero Club certificate (No.10) was Lancelot D. Gibbs. On 25 June 1910 he announced his intention of setting up an aviation school at Brooklands using a Sommer Biplane and a Henri Farman Biplane for instruction.

By January 1911 he was housed in shed No.17, together with the Universal Aviation Company, and was advertising tuition on monoplanes and biplanes for £75. However, there seems to have been little interest in the School and there is no record of any pupils having gained a certificate.

Gibbs was heavily involved with the construction and testing of the Universal Aviation Company's Birdling Monoplane.

THE DUCROCQ AND LAWFORD SCHOOL

1911-1913

The next school to arrive at Brooklands was that of Maurice Ducrocq and Bill Lawford, which was located in shed No.14 and commenced advertising at the beginning of 1911. Their equipment consisted of an Henri Farman Biplane and a Nieuport Monoplane.

At first they do not seem to have been very successful and it was not until 26 November 1912 that their first pupil gained his certificate. This was John Alcock, later to gain immortal fame as the first man to fly the Atlantic non-stop.

Two further certificates were awarded to their pupils before the School closed down early in 1913. One of these went to Percy M. Muller, later to become general manager of the Vickers factory at Weybridge.

THE DEPERDUSSIN SCHOOL

1911-1912

The pioneer French aircraft manufacturers, Deperdussin, commenced building aeroplanes in England and in the summer of 1911 they opened a flying school at Brooklands where they operated out of sheds Nos. 22 and 23.

The School was equipped with the handsome Deperdussin Monoplanes.

Tuition cost £75 including breakages and third party insurance. A £15 rebate was offered to any pupil who obtained his Royal Aero Club certificate without breakage or damage to machines.

DEPERDUSSIN Aviation School at Brooklands, thorough instruction in flying by competent staff; special terms to Army and Navy- Officers. For full particulars apply to THE BRITISH DEPER-DUSSIN AEROPLANE SYNDICATE, LTD., 30, Regent Street, Piccadilly Circus, S.W., or at Brooklands.

DEPERDUSSIN Aviation School at Brooklands; thorough instruction n flying by competent staff; thorough tuition £75, including breakages and third party insurance. Apply to THE BRITISH DEPERDUSSIN AEROPLANE SYNDICATE, LTD., 30, Regent Street, Piccadilly Circus, S.W., or at Brooklands.

The first certificate gained by a Deperdussin pupil went to J.D.P Chataway on 12 December 1911. Five more certificates were awarded to Deperdussin pupils before the School moved to Hendon in June 1912.

Their best known graduates were Captain Patrick Hastings (certificate No.194 on 12 March 1912) and R.L. Charteris (certificate No.197, also on 12 March 1912). Tragically, Patrick Hastings was killed in September 1912 when his Deperdussin broke up in the air over Graveley, near Hitchin.

Left: Monoplane produced by the British Deperdussin Aeroplane Co. of the type used at the Deperdussin School

THE

HERBERT SPENCER

SCHOOL

1911-1914

Some of the earliest British aviators were members of the Spencer family. The first to become an aeronaut was Edward Spencer who made his first balloon ascent in May 1836. His second son, Charles Green Spencer, named after his godfather, the celebrated Charles Green of *'Nassau'* balloon fame, was a keen balloonist and a champion bicyclist. Charles Green Spencer had 11 children, many of whom, both men and women, became well-known balloonists and parachutists and won many prizes.

HERBERT SPENCER FLYING SCHOOL, Brooklands Aerodrome, Weybridge. Thorough instruction on the Old Engine-behind Box-kite, still the best aeroplane in the world for learning to fly. Write for particulars.

The youngest son of this family was Herbert Spencer, born in 1884, who

became involved with the family firm manufacturing balloons and airships at Highbury and was engineer-pilot of the first airship to cross London. He then went on to the construction of aeroplanes, one of which was a virtual copy of the Farman Biplane. This he took to Brooklands and taught himself to fly on it.

At that time he occupied shed No.28. His efforts were rewarded when he gained his Royal Aero Club certificate (No.124) on 29 August 1911.

Blériot Monoplane outside the shed of the Herbert Spencer Flying School, the Flight Ticket Office is in the background

HERBERT SPENCER FLYING SCHOOL, Brooklands Aerodrome, Weybridge. Tuition and practical constructional work, £50. Passenger flights from £2 2s.

HERBERT SPENCER FLYING SCHOOL,
Brooklands Aerodrome, Weybridge.—Tuition
and practical constructional work from £40. Passenger
flights, from £2 2s.

He then set up the Herbert Spencer Flying School in shed No.9 and commenced advertising tuition in the aeronautical press. In March 1912 the charge for tuition and practical construction work was from £40, with passenger flights from £2.10; by February 1913 the tuition fee had risen to £50.

The Spencer School seems to have operated until early in 1914 but only one of their pupils actually gained a certificate (No.151) awarded to F.M. Ballard on 31 October 1911. Spencer used his Farman-type biplane and also a biplane reconstructed from the Macfie Biplane. Spencer also built a more sophisticated pusher biplane which was eventually sold to the Royal Flying Corps.

Herbert Spencer Biplane at Brooklands (rebuilt from Macfie Empress Biplane)

Herbert Spencer's
Farman-type Biplane
outside his shed

THE INTERNATIONAL CORRESPONDENCE SCHOOLS

1912

It was also possible to learn to fly (in theory) by correspondence course and the well-known firm, International Correspondence Schools, offered tuition by post in 1912. Eventually the pupil had to have some practical experience and I.C.S. operated a Blériot Monoplane from a number of aerodromes, including Brooklands.

The International Correspondence School's Blériot Monoplane

THE HOWARD FLANDERS SCHOOL

1912-1914

R L Howard Flanders, although disabled from birth, was one of A.V. Roe's earliest assistants and helped him with his first flights from Lea Marshes during the summer of 1909. He then joined J.V. Neale at Weybridge and designed the Pup monoplane.

F LANDERS SCHOOL.—Tuition on Monoplane with dual control.—For full particulars and terms, apply, L. HOWARD-FLANDERS, LTD., Brooklands Aerodrome, Weybridge.

In August 1910 he commenced the design and construction of a large monoplane which was eventually scrapped in May 1911 due to the non-availability of its 120 h.p. A.B.C. engine. He then designed and built the first of a series of handsome monoplanes, some of which were ordered for the Royal Flying Corps. The factory was at Townsend Terrace,

Sheen Road, Richmond and the aircraft were assembled in shed No.33 at Brooklands.

Early in 1912 a flying school was set up and the first advertisements appeared in *'Flight'* on 1 March 1912, when tuition was advertised in a monoplane with dual control. From about this time the School occupied shed No.12. Flanders' test pilots and instructors were Ronald C. Kemp and E.V.B. Fisher. The company and the School received a

The Flanders F.3 Monoplane

severe setback when Fisher and his passenger were killed when the Flanders F.3 Monoplane stalled on a climbing turn without sufficient height to recover.

Fisher, who was intimately concerned in A.V. Roe's earliest experiments, had been granted his certificate (No.77) on 2 May 1911 and had a considerable number of hours to his credit. He had worked with Howard Flanders, in the first permanent hangar to be erected at Brooklands, on the construction of the latter's first monoplane, and had been secretary of the original Shed-holders Committee and the Founder of the first Brooklands Aero Club. He had learned to fly on the Hanriot Monoplane at the Hanriot School and had also flown the Vickers-R.E.P. on which he had a serious crash and had then once more joined forces with his old

THE
FLANDERS MONOPLANE
60·80 H.P. Green Engine (Circuit of Britain Type).   One or two seaters.
Pupils taught on monoplane with double control.   £10 returned in event of no damage.
L. HOWARD-FLANDERS, Ltd., Brooklands, Weybridge.

TUITION
£75
INCLUSIVE

Above: The Flanders F.4 Monoplane at Brooklands

friend Howard Flanders on whose latest machine he met his death. This accident resulted in a very serious loss to British aviation. Fisher was a man who could ill be spared and the aircraft, which was destroyed by the fire which followed the smash, was a most promising machine.

It would seem that the bad publicity resulting from this and other monoplane crashes may have deterred pupils from joining the School and there is no record of any pilot's certificates having been awarded to anyone trained at the Flanders School. However, the School continued until the end of 1913, involved mainly in the test-flying of the Flanders Monoplanes and Biplane. Pilots included Freddie Raynham and Duckinfield Jones, and a pupil was C. Layzell-Apps.

Right: The Flanders F.3 Monoplane at Brooklands with early Marconi wireless apparatus installed.

THE VICKERS FLYING SCHOOL

1912-1914

The great British armaments conglomerate, Vickers Ltd., commenced the construction of aeroplanes in March 1911 at the Erith works of Vickers Sons and Maxim. The first flight of their No. 1 Monoplane was made from a field at Joyce Green, Dartford, in July 1911 and was then taken to Brooklands for further flight trials. Early in 1912, the Vickers Flying School was established at Brooklands in sheds Nos. 37/38/39 and 40 near the Byfleet banking on the west side of the Brooklands Motor Course. A further seven monoplanes, of similar design to the first machine, were

A Vickers monoplane in flight over the Vickers sheds at Brooklands Further Monoplanes and a Biplane are on the ground

Vickers Biplane and
Monoplanes outside the
Vickers sheds

produced by Vickers, several of which were used to train pupils at the Flying School.

Towards the end of 1912 three Farman-type pusher biplanes were purchased from Hewlett & Blondeau at Brooklands. These were known as the Vickers Boxkite and were extensively used for the initial training of pupils before they graduated to the more advanced monoplanes.

In December 1913 an equal-span version of the Boxkite was built by Vickers with an enclosed nacelle and side-by-side seating for the instructor and his pupil. It was known as the Vickers Pumpkin. A version of the Blériot Monoplane was also built.

Between 1912 and the outbreak of war in August 1914, the

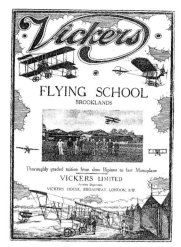

Vickers School trained 77 pupils, second only to the Bristol School at Brooklands.

R.H. Barnwell had been appointed chief flying instructor, with Archie Knight as one of his assistants. The first Royal Aero Club certificate (No.257)

Pupils and staff of the Vickers School in front of the Vickers No.5 Monoplane. In the centre, standing, is R.H.Barnwell, the chief instructor and on his right is Archie Knight, his assistant

was awarded to Captain C. Darbyshire on 24 July 1912. Two further sheds (Nos. 41 and 42) were occupied by Vickers at the beginning of 1913.

Several well-known pilots were trained at the Vickers School. These included Major W. Sefton Brancker (Certificate No.525), R.K. Pierson (No.660), Captain Hugh Dowding (No.711) and J. Lankester Parker (No.813).

The Vickers School, with its instructors and aircraft, was taken over by the Royal Flying Corps on the outbreak of war in August 1914.

Far Left: Vickers Biplane, built by Hewlett & Blondeau, outside the Vickers sheds with a group of pupils

Below: Vickers biplane at Brooklands

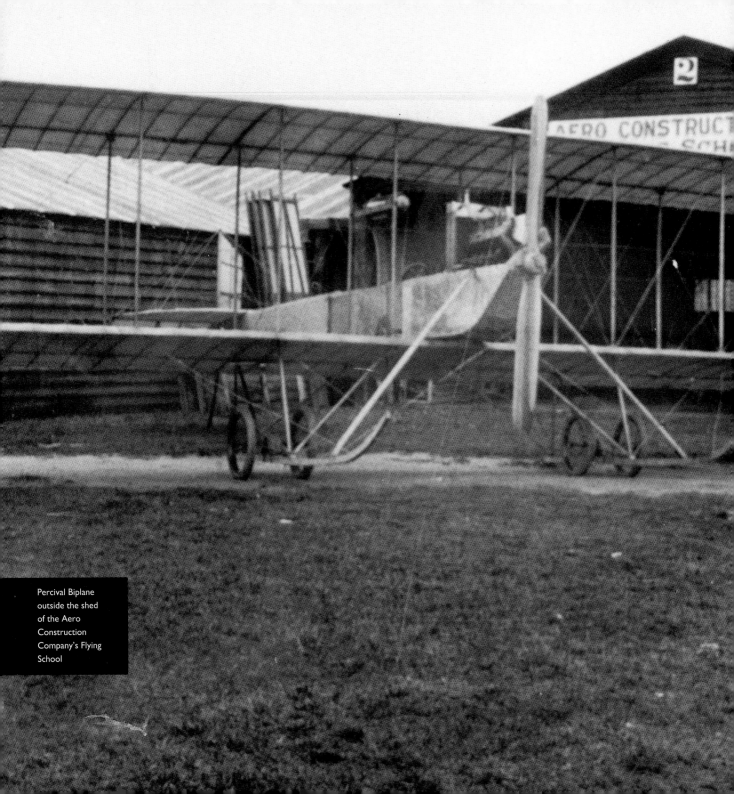

Percival Biplane
outside the shed
of the Aero
Construction
Company's Flying
School

THE
PERCIVAL FLYING
SCHOOL

(THE AERO CONSTRUCTION COMPANY)

1911-1913

The Aero Construction Company was set up by George Holt Thomas, one of the great founding fathers of the British aircraft industry; the first product was a biplane designed by N.S. Percival in conjunction with Percy Maxwell Muller.

In September 1911 the company set up a flying school, initially equipped with the Percival Biplane; subsequently they operated a Caudron Biplane.

The first and only Royal Aero Club certificate (No.390) awarded to one of their pupils was gained by G.N. Humphreys on 7 January 1913.

The company operated from shed No.2.

THE
SOPWITH SCHOOL

1912-1914

Thomas Octave Murdoch Sopwith made his début at Brooklands on 22 October 1910 with the Howard Wright Biplane which he had just purchased and which he crashed on his first attempt at flight. He subsequently bought a Howard Wright Monoplane and on 21 November 1910 he brought it out for the first time. After a period spent in taxiing on the ground, he then attempted some straight flights at

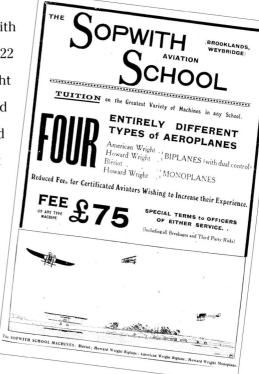

THE
SOPWITH (BROOKLANDS, WEYBRIDGE)
AVIATION
SCHOOL

TUITION on the Greatest Variety of Machines in any School.

FOUR
ENTIRELY DIFFERENT
TYPES of AEROPLANES

American Wright
Howard Wright } BIPLANES (with dual control)
Bleriot
Howard Wright } MONOPLANES

Reduced Fees for Certificated Aviators Wishing to Increase their Experience.

FEE
(ON ANY TYPE MACHINE)
£75
SPECIAL TERMS to OFFICERS OF EITHER SERVICE.
(Including all Breakages and Third Party Risks)

The SOPWITH SCHOOL MACHINES : Bleriot ; Howard Wright Biplane ; American Wright Biplane ; Howard Wright Monoplane.

TUITION.
THE SOPWITH AVIATION SCHOOL has the greatest variety of machines of any school in Great Britain. Tuition on Howard Wright or American-Wright Biplanes, with dual control, Blériot or Howard Wright Monoplanes. FOUR DISTINCT TYPES.—Particulars from the SOPWITH AVIATION SCHOOL, Brooklands, Weybridge.

low altitude. After lunch he made some circuits of Brooklands; later in the afternoon he qualified for his Royal Aero Club certificate and completed a successful day by taking up his first passenger in the evening. During this period he shared shed No.21 with Howard Wright.

During 1911 Sopwith continued his meteoric progress, winning prizes galore and becoming one of Britain's foremost test pilots.

The Burgess-Wright Biplane of the Sopwith School. The track and footbridge may be seen in the background

On his return from his most successful tour of America, Tom Sopwith opened his flying school at Brooklands on 1 February 1912. The initial equipment consisted of an American Burgess-Wright Biplane, a 70 h.p. Gnome Blériot Monoplane, a two year old Howard Wright Monoplane with 40 h.p. A.B.C. engine and the old *'Family Tank'* Howard Wright Biplane.

The first instructors were Tom Sopwith and Freddie Raynham.

Sopwith's Burgess-Wright biplane outside the Sopwith Shed.

The Howard Wright
Monoplane with a 40 h.p.
A.B.C. engine

The Howard Wright
Biplane with Tommy
Sopwith at the controls

The first Sopwith pupil to gain his Royal Aero Club certificate (No.207) was D.G. Young in the Burgess-Wright on 16 April 1912. By the end of October that year, ten more pupils had passed the tests for their certificates, including Major Hugh Trenchard (No.270) on 13 August, Harry G. Hawker (No.297) on 17 September and the aircraft constructor Howard T. Wright (No.331) on 15 October. All flew the Henri Farman Biplane which had been purchased in 1912. During this period, Sopwiths occupied sheds Nos. 29, 30 and 31.

The Sopwith School returned briefly to Brooklands in the spring of 1914 and two more pupils gained their certificates. The total number of Sopwith pupils who were awarded Royal Aero Club certificates was 13.

The Sopwith sheds at Brooklands - Nos. 29/31

THE

BLÉRIOT SCHOOL

1914

The Blériot School which had been established at Hendon in 1910 and had trained a succession of skilled monoplane pilots, opened a new school at Brooklands towards the middle of 1914. However, only two pupils had earned their aviators' certificates by the outbreak of war in August 1914.

A large Blériot factory had, of course, been established at Brooklands for several years and had built numerous aircraft including Blériot Monoplanes, Caudron Biplanes and Avro 504 Biplanes.

In 1914 they occupied sheds Nos. 1, 2, 26, 27 and 28.

During the approximately 4 years of flying schools at Brooklands prior to World War I, 318 pupils gained their Royal Aero Club certificates there. This was almost 50%

Blériot
Monoplar
outside th
Blériot sh
No. 3

Blériot School
instructor and pupil

of the total certificates gained in Britain during the period and easily disposes of the popular misconception that Hendon was the hub of all aerial activity in the country. Not only was Brooklands established first, but throughout the whole period it was the centre of three-quarters of the real work and effort behind British aviation.

   During the same period five pupils were killed in the course of their training at Brooklands, all but one of these accidents was due to stalling off a climbing turn. At the same time, fifteen Brooklands-trained pilots were killed in other parts of the country.

BROOKLANDS
IN THE
GREAT WAR

Britain declared war on Germany on 4 August 1914 and Brooklands, in common with other aerodromes, was immediately placed under military control. The Vickers, Bristol and Sopwith Flying Schools were turned over to the Royal Flying Corps and became the Military Training School. The last pre-war Royal Aero Club certificate (No.860) gained at Brooklands had been awarded to Lieutenant J.D.G. Sanders, flying a Bristol Boxkite of the Bristol School.

The Martinsyde and Blériot firms continued to build aeroplanes in their sheds at Brooklands and Sopwith machines were brought in from Kingston for assembly and test flying.

Very soon the Vickers company established a large factory on the site of the old Itala Motor Works on the east side of the aerodrome.

The first pilot's certificate (No.867) issued to a Military Flying School pupil was awarded to Norman Sholto Douglas flying a Bristol Boxkite, and up to the end of 1914, twenty one pilots obtained their certificates at the Military School. One of them was the great Frank Barnwell.

Brooklands gradually came more and more under the control of the military and various units were formed there before they went to France or to the Middle East. These included Nos. 1,8,9 and 10 Squadrons of the Royal Flying Corps. Flying training came under the control of Nos.2 and 23 Reserve Squadrons.

Maurice Farman S.7 Biplane at Brooklands outside the Blériot factory

Brooklands became a centre for wireless instruction.

A Wireless Experimental Flight was formed there in December 1915 and a Wireless School was established early in 1916 which became a Wireless and Observer School on 24 October 1916.

In the midst of all this military activity, the Blue Bird Cafe, which was being used as a canteen, was destroyed by fire on 28 March 1917.

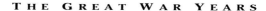

Royal Flying Corps Training Aircraft 1914-1918. Types used at Brooklands

No 2 Reserve Squadron
Maurice Farman Shorthorn
Maurice Farman Longhorn
B.E.2c
B.E.8
S.E.5a
Avro 504
Avro 508
Vickers F.B.5 Gunbus
Martinsyde S.1
Henry Farman
Blériot XI
Morane Monoplane

No 23 Reserve Squadon
B.E.2c
B.E.2e
B.E.12
Avro 504A
Avro 504J
D.H.6
Martinsyde Elephant
Sopwith Pup

Wireless & Observers' School
B.E.2
B.E 2e
R.E.7

A large Aircraft Acceptance Park was set up on 1 August 1917 and was renamed No.10 (Brooklands) A.A.P. on 12 October 1917; it was responsible for the assembly and test-flying of new aeroplanes received from the factories. These were mainly Sopwith and Vickers machines and S.E.5a fighters built at Vickers, Weybridge as well as aircraft built by Blériot Aeronautics and Martinsyde. The A.A.P. closed down early in 1920.

A great variety of aeroplanes was rapidly assembled at Brooklands for the use of pupils of the newly established Royal Flying Corps Reserve Aeroplane Squadrons.

B.E.8 Biplane at Brooklands during the Great War

BROOKLANDS SHRINKS THE WORLD

The unexpected end of the Great War in November 1918 found the Vickers Company with a very large order book for their Weybridge factory. This amounted to some 400 Vimy Bombers – these orders were almost immediately cut by 250 machines. This gave Vickers and all other aircraft manufacturers grave problems as there was, as yet, no proper civil aircraft requirement to counteract the loss of the military orders. Many firms went to the wall, or left the aircraft industry to seek orders for other products needed in the post-war world. Luckily for Vickers there were three prestigious aviation prizes on offer viz:

1. The Daily Mail prize offered before the War for the first non-stop flight across the Atlantic to a terminating point anywhere in the British Isles.

2. The Australian Government's offer of £10,000 for the first flight by

Australians from Britain to Australia to be completed within 30 days and before the end of 1919.

3. The South African Government's offer of £10,000 for the first flight by South Africans from Britain to Cape Town.

The talented Vickers team at Weybridge under the leadership of Percy Maxwell Muller, Archie Knight and Rex Pierson had all learnt to fly at Brooklands before the War at the Ducrocq and Lawford, Bristol & Vickers Schools respectively and their combined expertise helped to produce the remarkable Vimy bomber, which had such an impressive load-carrying capability that it was a natural choice as an entrant for the various long distance prize attempts.

A Vickers Vimy Bomber at Brooklands with Ross and Keith Smith and Sergeants Bennett and Shiers on board.

The Transatlantic machine was specially modified for the record attempt and was in fact the 13th Vimy to be built. The selected pilot Jack Alcock was also trained at Brooklands – at the Ducrocq & Lawford School where he gained his certficate in November 1912 and where he worked as a test pilot up to the outbreak of war in August 1914. He was one of the finest British pilots of the era.

Pilot Harry
Hawker

The story of how he and Arthur Whitten Brown conquered the Atlantic is too well-known to need retelling, but it highlighted the excellent long distance performance of the Vimy.

Two other Brooklands-trained pilots in Brooklands-assembled aeroplanes attempted in 1919 to make the first non-stop flight across the Atlantic. These were Harry Hawker (trained at the Sopwith School) in the Sopwith Rolls-Royce Atlantic and Freddie Raynham (trained at the Avro School) in the Martinsyde Raymor. Unfortunately both attempts were unsuccessful.

A second long distance Vimy, with provision for tropical stores and spare parts for the Australian flight was prepared at Weybridge (Brooklands) and was given one of the newly-introduced British civil aircraft markings – G-EAOU. The Australian Air Force crew had two pilots, the brothers Ross & Keith Smith & two mechanics Sergeants W.H. Shiers & J.M. Bennett; they left Hounslow on 12th November, 1919 and arrived in Darwin just under 28 days later on 10th December, 1919 after a series of difficulties which were manfully overcome.

The 75th anniversary of this epic flight was commemorated in September 1994 when a replica of G-EAOU, built in Australia and the U.S.A., flown by Peter McMillan and Lang Kidby and sponsored by National Geographic Magazine, Shell, Brooklands Museum and others, reproduced the first flight to Australia. The Vimy was called *"The Spirit of Brooklands"* (the Brooklands Museum logo) in recognition of the original machine's birthplace and was completed at Brooklands and flown from thence to Farnborough before setting out for Australia via the Middle East, India and Singapore. In spite of bad weather with strong headwinds and a forced landing in Indonesia due to an engine failure, the flight was completed successfully in about 42 days.

Vickers groundcrew at Newfoundland with Vimy

Following the success of this flight *"The Spirit of Brooklands"* may well attempt the Transatlantic crossing some time in the future.

The South African flight also used a Vickers Vimy standard military type named the "Silver Queen" and registered G-UABA. Piloted by Lt. Col. Pierre Van Ryneveld and Major C.J. Quintin Brand of the South African Air Force, the Vimy left Brooklands on 4th February, 1920. Unfortunately a leaking radiator caused the machine to crash at Korosko in Upper Egypt. A second Vimy was borrowed from the Royal Air Force in Egypt and named "Silver Queen II." This one reached

Bulawayo in Southern Rhodesia but had to retire due to a damaged engine. The flight was completed in a borrowed D.H.9. The crew shared the £10,000 prize and were knighted by King George V.

Meanwhile Vickers had developed and were building what has been called *'the true father of all airliners'.* This was the Vimy Commercial which utilised the wings and tail assembly of the Vimy bomber with a new roomy and unobstructed fuselage of wooden monocoque construction. It was an instant success and a production line was laid down at Brooklands, one of the first sales being an order for 40 machines for China. The Commercial was the forerunner of a series of large biplanes which kept the Brooklands factory and airfield busy until the mid 1930's.

The Vimy Commercial prototype K-107 (later G-EAAV) also made an attempt on the South African first flight. The pilots were S.P. (Stan) Cockerell, who learnt to fly at the Bristol School in 1911 and Tommy Broome. Both were Vickers test pilots.

Vickers second successful post war design was a single-engined biplane amphibian the Viking, which had seats for four passengers. The Vikings were built and flown at Brooklands and by tragic coincidence Sir John Alcock and Sir Ross Smith and Sgt. Bennett were all killed in crashes involving the Viking.

These commercial activities kept the Brooklands aerodrome open and active and kept together a workforce of skilled aeronautical engineers and craftsmen who were able to assist in the setting up of the flying schools, clubs and engineering facilities at Brooklands, when civilian aviation *'took off'* in the mid 1920's.

The famous flying duo of J. Alcock and A. Whitten-Brown

POST WAR BROOKLANDS

T he Great War ended on 11 November 1918 but it took nearly a year for the various military units to leave the Brooklands site. The damage caused to the track and roads by the heavy military vehicles delayed the re-opening of the race track until 1920 and the first race took place on 11 April of that year. The airfield was in good condition and the first civilian organisation to return to Brooklands in 1919 and 1920 was run by Colonel G.L.P. Henderson who refurbished an Armstrong-Whitworth F.K.8, a Fairey IIIa and a Fairey IIIc for eventual export to Sweden. In 1924 and 1925, Southern Counties Aviation Company operated Avro 504Ks on passenger-carrying flights.

A Brooklands Aero Club was operating in 1923/1924 but appears to have been a short-lived venture.

Avro 504K of the Southern Counties Aviation Company used at Brooklands for passenger flights

Avro 548 of the
Henderson School

The first Post war flying school at Brooklands was the Henderson School of Flying, opened in May 1926. Captain H. Duncan Davis joined it as Chief Flying Instructor. He had learned to fly in 1915 and had spent two years with a fighter squadron in France. He was then posted to the School of Special Flying at Gosport, under the command of Lieut. Colonel R.R. Smith-Barry, where the first really modern methods of flying training were put into practice. After demobilisation, he purchased a surplus Avro 504K and started joy-riding flights at Hamble aerodrome. In 1920 he moved to Margate and in 1921 became the Manager of Avro Transport. Later in 1921 he gave up flying as a profession and took over a partnership in a welding business in London. In May 1926 he joined Colonel Henderson at Brooklands and together they set up the Henderson School. The School owned nine Avro 548 Biplanes, six of which they built from ex-military Avro 504K spares and fitted with 80 h.p. Renault engines. Although used primarily for instructional work, during the summer they went to coastal resorts such as Skegness and Canvey Island to give joy-riding flights. On 20th September 1928, the School had its first fatal accident when Margaret Honor Welby crashed in G-EBFM. Shortly after this sad event, and following two successful years, Colonel Henderson

Instructor and two pupils
of the Henderson School
in front of an Avro 548

decided to retire and a band of enthusiasts, staff and pupils headed by Duncan Davis clubbed together to purchase the School, which was then renamed the Brooklands School of Flying.

The directors were Duncan Davis, H.S. Hamilton (Secretary) and Rivers Oldmeadow. Of the initial £3,000 capital, £2,200 went to Colonel Henderson and £300 was used for office furniture. Captain E.A. Jones and Major C.M. Pickthorn, together with Duncan Davis, were the initial instructors.

The Press reported:

"On Friday, 9 November, the newly-formed Brooklands School of Flying Ltd. was officially opened and despite very bad weather for the first week results were shown; Mrs. W.B. Scott, the racing motorist, and Mr. G.P. Kerr completed their first solos in perfect style. Three new pupils were welcomed, namely Mr. W.T. D'Eyncourt, Mr. E.L. Donner (Guards' Club) and Mr. C.S. Burney, the racing motor cyclist.

The School held an "At Home" at Brooklands on Sunday, 18 November, which was a great success. An interesting programme was given

D.H. 60X Moth
belonging to
Colonel Henderson

The opening of the Brooklands Aero Club on 17 May 1930. The Vickers Virginia Bomber in the foreground is surrounded by visiting aircraft

with the assistance of many pilots and private owners who included Miss W. Spooner on her Gipsy Moth; Capt. G. de Havilland on a Coupé Moth (Gipsy), Capt. H. Broad on a Gipsy Moth, Capt. F.E. Guest and Capt. Rodney who arrived on the former's Junkers monoplane, Flying Officer Summers and Flt.Lt. E.R. Scholefield, etc.

The programme opened with an exhibition flight by Capt. H.D. Davis A.F.C. and then Capt. H. Broad gave a fine display of aerobatics on his Gipsy Moth. Lieut.-Col. Henderson flew a Mono-Avro to show how such a machine can be flown.

Many guests were taken up for joy rides on the School machines piloted by Capt. H.D. Davis and Major Pickthorn, Capt. de Havilland (Coupé Moth), Col. Strange (Simmonds "Spartan") and Col. Henderson (Mono Avro) also helped."

Avro 504K of the Brooklands School of Flying

The initial equipment consisted of some of the Avro 548s and three Avro 504Ks, and by April 1929 the Avro 548s had been disposed of and replaced by the purchase of five de Havilland Gipsy and Cirrus Moths.

During 1929, over 200 hours of instructional flights were given at Brooklands and more than 40 pupils took their '*A*' licences.

Although Colonel Henderson had severed his connection with the Brooklands School of Flying, he had continued to fly from Brooklands and his death in the crash of a Junkers F.13 in July 1930 was a great shock to everyone.

The Brooklands Aero Club was reformed in May 1930 by the Brooklands Automobile Racing Club with one metal de Havilland Gipsy Moth (G-AASZ) and with Percy Bradley as Manager. A second Gipsy Moth (G-ABYI) was purchased in 1932.

In March 1931 Brooklands Aviation Ltd. was formed with Percy Bradley, Duncan Davis, Fred Sigrist and E.A. Jones as directors. Tragically Captain Jones was killed in a crash at Hendon on 8 November 1931.

Top Left: Avro 504K belonging to Colonel G.L.P. Henderson

Middle Left: Avro 548 of the Henderson School at Brooklands with some of the pupils and ground crew

Bottom Left: Metal de Havilland Gipsy Moth belonging to The Brooklands Aero Club

In 1931, Brooklands School of Flying replaced its remaining Cirrus Moths with Gipsy Moths. The College of Aeronautical Engineering opened at Brooklands in October 1931 and in 1932 it formed its own Flying Club, using Brooklands School of Flying aeroplanes.

The Brooklands School of Flying commenced a programme of expansion in 1932 when it took over the Cinque Ports Flying Club at Lympne on 1 January. The Brooklands Aero Club also started expanding in 1932 when they commenced a series of Sunday evening lectures in January

Below: The hangars of Brooklands Aviation Ltd. and the Brooklands School of Flying
In the background on the right is the infamous sewage farm
Below right: The hangar of the College of Aeronautical Engineering at Brooklands

Left: The 1932 Aero Clubhouse

and opened a Club shop in the spring. On 28 May 1932, the magnificent new Aero Clubhouse was opened. Designed by Graham Dawbarn in typical 1930's style, it became the pattern for aerodrome buildings throughout the world.

The Press Aero Club opened at Brooklands in 1932, with membership open to journalists and other pressmen.

Early in 1933, Brooklands Flying Club was set up by Brooklands Aviation Ltd. with Duncan Davis and Bill Massey as Directors and Captain Bush as Secretary. Captain Ian Mackenzie was Chief Flying Instructor and by 1934 they had five Gipsy Moths. Also in 1933, Brooklands Airways Ltd. was formed by buying out Personal Flying Services Ltd. They operated a Junkers F.13 and a de Havilland Puss Moth for taxi and charter work.

BROOKLANDS is the HEADQUARTERS of the PRESS AERO CLUB

Membership open to Journalists and Press - men
Sub.: 3 guineas p.a.

Free use of Club-House; and beneficial charges for all classes of flying and flying instruction.

WRITE TO THE SECRETARY c/o BROOKLANDS AERODROME

A group of Moth
instructors and pupils
outside the old Flying
Village sheds

Brooklands School of Flying expanded further in January 1933 when it took over the Northampton Aero Club at Sywell. By December 1933, Brooklands Aero Club had 550 members.

George Lowdell, Chief Instructor of the Brooklands School of Flying, resigned in February 1934 on his appointment as test pilot for Wolseley Motors.

In June 1934 the Masonic Country and Flying Club was opened at Brooklands and its members had the use of the tennis courts of the B.A.R.C. Ken Waller was appointed Chief Instructor of Brooklands School of Flying in May 1935.

The large hangar used by Brooklands Aviation Ltd. was destroyed by fire in October 1936, together with six aeroplanes housed inside. New hangars were completed in October 1937.

On 1 December 1937, the Brooklands Aero Club and Brooklands Flying Club were merged under the management of Brooklands Aviation Ltd. Until then, the Flying Club and School of Flying operated by Brooklands Aviation had been concerned with flying instruction at Brooklands, Lympne and Sywell, whereas the Aero Club, owned by the proprietors of the motor course and aerodrome, managed the Clubhouse and its social activities.

The Brooklands Aviation
Ltd. hangar on fire in
October 1936

With the start of the rearmament in Britain, No.11F Squadron of the Air Defence

Cadet Corps was established at Brooklands with the assistance of Brooklands Aviation Ltd. It remained on the Brooklands site until 1990 when it then moved to the grounds of Brooklands College.

George Lowdell - Chief Flying Instructor, Brooklands School of Flying

Whilst training under the Civil Air Guard scheme was not carried out at Brooklands, potential members were enrolled there and training was carried out at the South Coast Flying Club at Shoreham and at Northampton Aero Club, both part of the Brooklands Aviation Group.

With the outbreak of World War II imminent, the final flying club event at Brooklands was held on 20 August 1939.

When war was declared on 3 September, flying training ceased at Brooklands, although the Northampton Club became an Elementary Flying Training School for the Royal Air Force. The airfield and buildings at Brooklands were given over to the construction, repair and test-flying of Vickers and Hawker aircraft. Many of the Brooklands staff and pupils became members of the Air Transport Auxiliary and throughout the War they ferried Wellingtons and Hurricanes from Brooklands to the operational units of the R.A.F.

Virtually all visual evidence of pre-war flying at Brooklands has now disappeared, with the exception of the 1911 Flight Ticket Office and the 1932 Aero Clubhouse – not a great memorial to a site which was the most important centre for flying training in Britain for 30 years.

SOUTHERN COUNTIES AVIATION COMPANY

Avro 504K	G-EASG

Henderson Flying School

Avro 548	G-EAJB	G-EBFM	G-EBAJ	G-EBRD
	G-EBSC	G-EBVE	G-EBWH	G-EBWJ
Avro 504K	G-EBYE	G-AAFJ		
Boulton & Paul P.9	G-EASJ			
Henderson HSF.1	G-EBVF			

BROOKLANDS SCHOOL OF FLYING

Avro 548	G-EBVE	G-EBWJ	G-AADT	
Avro 504K	G-EBYE	G-AACA	G-AAEM	
D.H.60	G-EBPR			
D.H.60G	G-AALW	G-ABWN		
D.H.60X	G-EBUX	G-EBWA	G-EBZE	G-EBZH
	G-AAKK	G-ABAO		
Westland Widgeon	G-EBRM			
Simmonds Spartan	G-AAWM			

BROOKLANDS AERO CLUB

D.H.60G	G-AASZ	G-ABYB

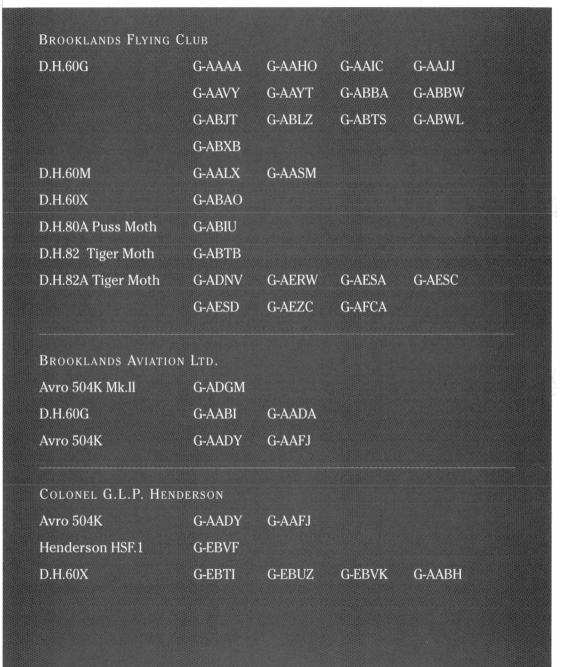

Brooklands Flying Club

D.H.60G	G-AAAA	G-AAHO	G-AAIC	G-AAJJ
	G-AAVY	G-AAYT	G-ABBA	G-ABBW
	G-ABJT	G-ABLZ	G-ABTS	G-ABWL
	G-ABXB			
D.H.60M	G-AALX	G-AASM		
D.H.60X	G-ABAO			
D.H.80A Puss Moth	G-ABIU			
D.H.82 Tiger Moth	G-ABTB			
D.H.82A Tiger Moth	G-ADNV	G-AERW	G-AESA	G-AESC
	G-AESD	G-AEZC	G-AFCA	

Brooklands Aviation Ltd.

Avro 504K Mk.II	G-ADGM	
D.H.60G	G-AABI	G-AADA
Avro 504K	G-AADY	G-AAFJ

Colonel G.L.P. Henderson

Avro 504K	G-AADY	G-AAFJ		
Henderson HSF.1	G-EBVF			
D.H.60X	G-EBTI	G-EBUZ	G-EBVK	G-AABH

Above: A D.H.60G of the Brooklands Flying Club after crashing into a D.H.60X of the Brooklands School of Flying in 1931

Above right: D.H.60G Gipsy Moth in the Brooklands Aviation hangar

D.H.82A Tiger Moth flying over an E.R.A. and M.G.

D.H Moth of
The Brooklands
Flying Club

BROOKLANDS
FLYING
CLUB

BROOKLANDS TODAY

A selection of letterheaded paper from 1930s Flying Schools and Clubs

Happily all is not lost. For the past 10 years a splendid new museum of aviation and motorsport has been rising like a phoenix from the ashes of the old Brooklands. Hardly a day goes by without some historic item being given to the Museum.

These donations range from a giant Vickers VC10 airliner to a vintage Tiger Moth and down to a flying helmet or even a ticket for a flight round Brooklands in the 1930's. Plans are nearing fruition for a vast new hangar to house the Museum's collection of 40 aircraft together with some 40,000 photographs and an impressive selection of aviation memorabilia.

Truly, Brooklands lives again.

Some recent aircraft visitors to Brooklands.

Top Left: Zlin Monoplane

Middle Left: De Havilland D.H. 85 Leopard Moth with the Sultan of Oman's Vickers VC10 in the background

Above: D.H. Gipsy Moth

Left: Replica Vickers Vimy carrying out trials at Brooklands prior to its epic flight to Australia

APPENDIX A

Apart from the serious matter of learning to fly and to repair the results of the numerous crashes, there was a lighter side to Brooklands as these extracts from Mrs. Hilda Hewlett's unpublished autobiography show very clearly. They portray a light-hearted acceptance of the hardships and long hours spent by the pupils and the instructors in their eagerness to take advantage of every moment of suitable flying weather:

"We had thought out no plans for the future, as we had to fly first. Business just came to us, we had great hopes that we could pay our way, we were absolutely dependent on one machine for pupils, passengers, and any prizes for flying. This caused us to live in a state of perpetual anxiety in case the least accident should happen to our one asset. It made me nervous of trying it, every time a pupil took it alone, we stood white and trembling for the consequences. Finally we decided to build another machine, save every penny to buy another Gnome, and so put our School on a safer footing. We lost no time, we ordered from France what we could not make ourselves, we worked harder and longer. We bought an acetylene welding plant, with which Gustave did wonders. That paid for itself in no time, it was the first

of its kind in England: not only aviators and aeroplane constructors came to have parts welded, but motorists came with broken axles, rods, and even parts of engines. They seemed to think anything could be mended, even the most impossible things, by this new invention. We turned the small case into a store, ordered all kinds of accessories from France and sold them to the ever increasing constructors who arrived on the track followed by the most weird contraptions. Farman gave us a licence to construct, Gustave was not content only to copy, he wanted to make a lighter machine with less wing surface. At night he worked out his designs, covering the floor of the one sitting room with chalk curves and measurements, over which he crawled and wrote minute figures aided by a slide rule.

We had pupils who were as keen as ourselves, their enthusiasm was a by-word on the track. One boy in the Navy walked from Walton, 8 miles or so, at 4 a.m. for his lessons. He threw stones at my window, I came down in scanty attire and made tea for all who were going to fly.

Another boy, who was at Aldershot, motor-biked from there every afternoon, got an evening lesson, slept in the big case which stood outside our hangar, had another lesson at break of day, returning to Aldershot in time for his duties at 8 a.m. Snowden-Smith became our most accomplished pupil and made the first cross-country flight, although he had fewer lessons than any other. He entered for the Brooklands to Brighton race and did it in better time than any biplane, but having passed a pylon on the wrong side, he was disqualified, which was a sad blow to him and to us. His ease and style of flying with such a low powered engine was quite like

Effimoff at Mourmelon. I often watched him in the early morning, he played about like a happy porpoise, he only lived to fly. Then I went up and tried to copy him ...

Another pupil push-biked from London every weekend, camped out anywhere, got as many lessons as possible, biking back early on Monday.

They were nearly all devoted to our hangar and our work, they spent their holidays and spare time with us, doing any jobs however dirty or hard, sharing our extremely primitive meals, filling our lives with perpetual fun and jokes. Not only did they work on aeroplanes, they washed up plates, cooked food, cleaned the bath, which we had bought and put in our cottage: it was a very great luxury to many who lived anywhere and anyhow on the track.

Gustave was a born teacher, his patience knew no bounds. He carefully studied each pupil, found out his faults and used his good qualities, advising, explaining and illustrating them in the machine, in consequence not one had an accident when he took the machine alone for the first time. It was counted a miracle in those days when machine after machine crashed, and pupils kicked their heels for weeks waiting for repairs. Every outsider put it down to luck, I put it down to a good teacher!

One very exciting moment for Gustave was when a pupil had the pilot's place and he sat beside him (dual control was, of course, not invented), the pupil got nervous and made a bad mistake, Gustave caught hold of the joy-stick to correct it, the boy held hard in fright and would not let go. Gustave had to give him a hard blow on his knuckles, just in time to right the machine and save a crash.

That life was worth living amongst men, young and old, who lived with one

aim, fearing not death, caring not for other things, respecting not overmuch law and regulation that stood in their way. The toil they did was prodigious, besides the brain work which had then no known rules to work on. The hours they worked were not reckoned, only the job in hand counted. The clothes they wore were mended with string or copper wire, socks and ties were seldom seen near a hangar. The food they existed on was chiefly tea, bread and butter, eked out with tinned stuff. No drinks, seldom a bottle of beer, much more tobacco than food. In summer they swam in the Wey, otherwise there was a minimum of washing. Many slept in the hangars or in huge packing cases outside. I made friends with most of them, being the only woman there they were ready to do anything to help me. We lived a curious communal life, with aviation shop talked day and night, in season and out of season.

The day came when I took the machine alone. I was nervous of hurting it. 'Whatever you do, don't go near those lumps where the house is pulled down, nor to the sewage farm' – those were Gustave's last injunctions. I made up my will I would not, yet I went straight into the old bricks and there stuck. They had a horrid attraction I could not overcome. I started again and flew. Soon after that the time came to take my ticket. I did not feel a bit nervous then, only very happy. Early one morning the R.A.C. representatives were on the ground, they all wanted to 'pass' me. I did the simple necessary turns, altitude and landing tests. Everyone was so glad and happy. We all went mad at that early hour and forgot even breakfast. All day long I had telegrams and for a week letters of congratulation. All the scoffers took back their words generously and fully. I was sent the most amusing lot of presents besides the

ordinary ones, and my dream was fulfilled. I was duly photographed and inter-viewed and patted on the back.

The Coronation provided a holiday and some happenings while we were at Brooklands. Some loyal aviators were to celebrate it by flying at night with a car searchlight tied on to a biplane for glory. I went to London to a seat in the Automobile Club to see the procession, with my family. I came on to the track about 10.30 a.m. to beg a lift to Weybridge station. There was a Panhard car of the 'Garden of Eden' date used to cut the grass on the aerodrome. For fear of accidents the blades were removed when not in use, and for fear of interfering aviators the start-ing handle was removed and hidden.

Being a holiday, many Brooklanders felt happy and gay. Twelve climbed into the old car and started the engine by pushing it in first speed. It just went about 6 m.p.h., but it proceeded with force and decision making direct for the doors of the hangars. All twelve men on board tried to do something, but too many aviators spoiled the driving, they went slowly and deliberately through the woodwork, wiping off a few passengers as the doors fell slowly apart with much creaking and cracking noise. It still went on right into a half-finished machine standing before it. There at last it was pulled up and stood as if looking at what it had done. The owner of the hangar, and also the designer of the aeroplane, were on it, and their language was worse than any I had ever heard. One man was literally rolling on the ground with laughter, while the others joined in. They kindly offered to take me to the station in it – I wisely declined.

That was only the beginning of Brooklands holiday. The evening ended by shooting, and not a single pane of glass round the hangars was whole by daybreak. A tiny house called 'The Bird-cage' was just then occupied by unpopular people. They were also unwise. The male occupier undressed before the window without drawing the blind. A huge acetylene headlight was directed on him from the garden. He got a pistol and shot at it. From all sides came answering shots till not a pane of glass was left whole. The big light was not affected, it burned steadily on. The lady inside had hysterics and very wisely left the house where she had no moral right to be and did not wish to be found. The light was then removed. Again I was blamed, but again I had been all day in town. After that, 'they' either believed me or thought me too good to escape. I told 'them' I was as 'an elder sister to the aviators', an example of good behaviour and preacher of reform, that I was cruelly misunderstood, and that if they wanted my help and influence they had not gone the right way to get it. This letter had a most curious effect, for I was from then treated quite differently."

The original Flying School buildings at Brooklands

APPENDIX B

BROOKLANDS, BYFLEET, SURREY

1. Controlling Authority.—Brooklands Estate Co., Brooklands Aerodrome, Byfleet, Surrey.

2. Landing Area

(a) *Dimensions.*—

N.—S.	1,000 yards.
N.E.—S.W.	900 yards.
E.—W.	650 yards.
S.E.—N.W.	450 yards.

(b) *Altitude above Mean Sea Level.*—50 feet (15 metres).

(c) *Surface conditions.*—Grass covered. The N. portion is somewhat rough.

3. Obstructions Requiring Special Caution

(a) *East side.*—Wooded hill, 200 feet high, 1 mile distant.

(b) *South side.*—Banked motor track, 20 feet high.

Note.—(i) A flying school is operated at the aerodrome and visiting aircraft should exercise due caution.

4. Special Signals

(1) A flashing neon light in the form of the letter " R " may be displayed on the roof of the N. hangar on the W. side of the aerodrome. When the sign is illuminated, all circuits must be right handed.

5. Lighting

(1) *Beacon.*—

    (a) *When operated.*—Irregular (under R.A.F. control).

    (b) *Character and period.*—Red ; flashing the morse letters OE (— — — •) approx. every 10 secs.

    (c) *Normal range.*—7 miles.

    (d) *Situation.*—Mobile.

    (e) *Overall height.*—(i) Above ground level : 5 feet (1·5 metres). (ii) Above sea level : 55 feet (17 metres).

6. Facilities for Aircraft

(1) *Refuelling.*—Aviation fuel, oil and fresh water available.

(2) *Repairs.*—Repairs can be executed by arrangement with Brooklands Aviation, Ltd.

(15535)—32

BROOKLANDS, BYFLEET, SURRE

6. Facilities for Aircraft—*continued*

(3) *Hangars.*—

Number.	Structure.	Net Breadth.	Net Depth.	Door Height.	D W.
		ft.	ft.	ft. in.	
Two ..	Brick and asbestos, in 2 bays	160	170	20 10	
One ..	Brick and asbestos, in 3 bays	240	170	20 10	

7. Facilities for Personnel

(1) *Transport.*—West Weybridge railway station, ⅓ mile. Garages or and at Weybridge.

(2) *Hotels, etc.*—Weybridge. Restaurant and sleeping accommodation Club House.

8. Local Regulations

(1) The direction of circuits must be right-handed when the wind is S. to W. and left-handed when from W. through N. to E. (above).

(2) When there is no wind, aircraft should land and take-off tow

Note.—The W. boundary of the " controlled zone " (*see* Part the E. of the aerodrome.

PRIVATE AERODROME

BROOKLANDS, BYFLEET, SURREY

Classification :

Telegrams :
" Aviation
Byfleet."

Telephone :
Byfleet 436.

Scale of ½ Inch to 1 Mile = 1:126,720

Lat. 51° 21' N. Long. 0° 28' W.

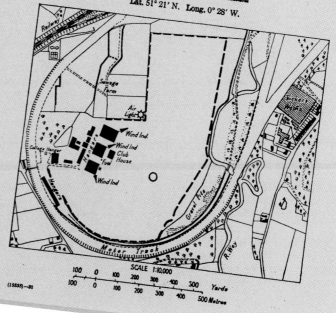

SCALE 1:10,000

(15535)—31

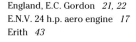

INTRODUCTORY FLIGHT OFFERS

'FIXED WING' AIRCRAFT

THE 'DOUBLE'

Two instructional flights landing away – one hour total

THE 'FLYING START'

Four x 1 hour P.P.L. lessons at a special price

HELICOPTER

THE LIFT OFF

One hour package – 30 minutes 'hands-on' flying

LONDON SIGHTSEEING TOUR

Half hour tour by helicopter flies you along the Thames at 1000 ft.

Ring 0181-953 4411 to enquire about these special offers.

By sending us this voucher, you will be entitled to £10 off any one of the above.

(please note: not all flights are available from each location)

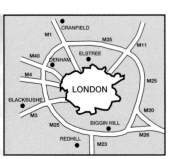

Current Cabair Flying Schools operate at: Biggin Hill, Blackbushe, Cranfield, Denham, Elstree and Redhill

CABAIR
FLYING SCHOOLS

HEAD OFFICE: THE CABAIR GROUP LTD, ELSTREE AERODROME, BOREHAMWOOD, HERTS WD6 3AW

£10 VOUCHER

TOWARDS YOUR FIRST FLIGHT IN A 'FIXED WING' AIRCRAFT OR A HELICOPTER

This Voucher is only redeemable against any one of the Flight Offers stated opposite.

CABAIR
FLYING SCHOOLS

BROOKLANDS
'FLYING START' BOOK